Mobilize

© 2014 Kingdom Mobilization

ISBN: ISBN 978-0-9916-5800-8

Published by Kingdom Mobilization, Inc., April 1, 2014, Estero, Florida, USA

Kingdom Mobilization
20041 South Tamiami Trail, Suite 1
Estero, Florida, USA 33928
www.kingmo.org

About the Authors

George Peter Gundlach
Managing Director,
Kingdom Mobilization, Inc.

George Peter Gundlach is the Managing Director of Kingdom Mobilization, Inc. He has served in senior management and marketing positions in both businesses and ministries. He is an accomplished strategic planner and communicator. Mr. Gundlach is a graduate of the University of Florida.

In addition to his work for Kingdom Mobilization, he is an accomplished writer and blogger. His monthly newsletter *Plan to Grow* focuses on helping both people and organizations to prosper. Mr. Gundlach's greatest passion is to see people discover and engage in the calling for which they are destined.

George's wife Nancy is a licensed landscape architect and a certified land planner. He is also the father of seven very exceptionally motivated children who serve in a variety of capacities including ministry, the arts, and medicine.

Charles Nolen Rollins
Founder & President
Kingdom Mobilization, Inc.

Charles Nolen Rollins is founder and President of Kingdom Mobilization, Inc. (See www.kingmo.org) He also serves as the Lead Pastor/Coach of Legacy Church in Estero, Florida and as a consultant for ministries around the world.

Nolen has forty years plus of experience in pastoral ministry and world missions. He has previously served on the staff of churches in Tennessee, Kentucky, Oklahoma, Georgia, Arkansas, and Florida. He has served as Executive Pastor of several large churches including First Baptist Church, Atlanta, Georgia for eight years and First Baptist Church, Naples, Florida for four years.

He is a long time student and teacher of leadership development. He has led leadership conferences and served as a leadership development consultant for several churches, denominational organizations, mission agencies, other non-profit organizations, Christian schools, and businesses.

Nolen is a graduate of the University of Tennessee, Tennessee Temple Theological Seminary, and the Southern Baptist Theological Seminary.

Nolen and Clarice, his wife of over forty years, have two daughters and six grandchildren.

Table of Contents:

Where there is no vision,
the people perish...
Proverbs 29:18 (KJV)

Chapter 1
Mobilization Starts with a Dream and a Vision

The stories of people who started with nothing except a dream and a vision are legendary. Sam Walton milked cows and sold newspapers before starting Walmart. J.K. Rowling was on welfare before creating the Harry Potter Series. Ingvar Kamprad lived in a small Swedish village before starting IKEA. Howard Schultz grew up in a Brooklyn Project before starting Starbucks. Ursula Burns grew up in a Manhattan East Side Project before running Xerox. Each one envisioned a good future even though they started with little.

As you ponder the idea of starting a mobilization movement where you live, you need to begin with a clear understanding of the importance of vision. Vision is a picture of what we dream the future will look like. It is a reality that we anticipate and a belief about what should be. While organizations and individuals have engaged in strategic planning for some time, the issue of vision is a more recent discovery. We have learned that when we also focus on vision that strategy becomes better and plans succeed.

Michael Hyatt wrote an article describing his journey of taking a struggling company from an "ash heap" to a place of success. He acknowledges his natural bent to think too small. He says,

> "Through the years, I had learned that if you think about strategy (the how) too early, it will actually inhibit your vision (the what) and block you from thinking as big as you need to think. The problem is that people get stuck on the how. They don't see how they could accomplish more, so they throttle back their vision, convinced that they must be realistic."

Taking Hyatt's advice, to dream big we need to discipline ourselves to focus more on the what instead of the how. The level of discipline to do so varies from person to person depending on their personality type. As an example, we have to be very disciplined because we are strategic thinkers. We have to resist the temptation to jump prematurely to strategy.

When we coach mobilizers and others on the importance of vision, we tell them to start their visionary thoughts with the words "I see/…" or "I envision/…" These words are then followed by vision thoughts that are:

- Intense – Vision invokes strong feelings.
- Personal – Vision is unique to the one envisioning.
- Vivid – Vision often takes on the properties of a clear mental picture.
- Passionate – Vision is something that we feel we must do.

Stepping back and contemplating vision has birthed businesses, started great philanthropic works and helped people understand their own personal life missions. Jonathan Swift wrote, "Vision is the art of seeing what is invisible to others." We have found this process to be nothing short of POWERFUL!

The GPS Life Journey curriculum (which we will discuss at length in chapter seven) states, "Your vision is usually a series of descriptive (specific and clear) bullet points or statements, rather than one long narrative." The example is used of someone who felt called to mentor troubled teenage boys and describes his vision bullet points like this:

- I envision being trained on how to mentor young men.
- I envision building strong, healthy relationships with troubled teenage boys.
- I envision a multiplying effect as many of these boys will mentor others in the future.

Do you know what 15 year-old Malala and the Profit Nehemiah have in common with people that seek to mobilize others? Their visions were challenged and yours will likely be as well. We have seen all too frequently people with vision face serious opposition. Vision has a way of making controlling people nervous and insecure people angry.

A most recent example of opposition is 15-year old Malala Yousafzai, the Pakistani teenager shot in the head by the Taliban, for promoting "Western thinking." Thankfully she recovered and has courageously returned to school. She is not alone. Only a few hundred years ago scientists were threatened with retribution, even death, for envisioning "ridiculous" things like the earth being round, and that the sun was at the center of our solar system. Author Chuck Swindoll asserts, "You haven't really led until you have become familiar with the stinging barbs of the critic. For the leader, opposition is inevitable."

We can also learn much about vision from a study of Nehemiah, the fifth century high official in the Persian court of King Artaxerxes I. His vision was for the restoration of the city of Jerusalem, which during its history was destroyed twice, besieged 23 times, attacked 52 times, and captured and recaptured 44 times. Nehemiah's story has at its core every element related to vision. He envisioned rebuilding the wall surrounding the city that had been destroyed by an invader and left in shambles by apathetic citizens. In the Bible, in the Book of Nehemiah we see:

- Vision Formed – He was compelled to rebuild the wall.
- Vision Shared – He asked the king for permission to do so.
- Vision Acted On – He organized others to help him in the task.
- Vision Resisted – The "good old boy" network mocked him and tried to stop him.
- Vision Completed – Jerusalem's walls stood once again.

Jack Welch, the former head of General Electric (who worked his way up from the shop floor to lead one of America's most successful companies) says it this way, "Good … leaders create a vision, articulate the vision, passionately own the vision, and relentlessly drive it to completion."

When you were a child and young adult I suspect you used to dream a lot about the future. Then, without realizing it, your dreaming and envisioning tapered off. Why do we stop dreaming and having vision? Comedian George Carlin speculated one reason when he said, "Some people see things that are and ask, why? Some people dream of things that never were and ask, why not? Some people have to go to work and don't have time for all that." I believe Carlin had it right. It is the obligations and pressures of life that crowd out our dreams.

Dreaming about starting a mobilization movement produces a vision of the future. Vision is about where you are going and how people can be better off and the world a better place. Vision is filled with passion which brings great excitement and a sense of anticipation into your life. If it has been neglected, it may start slowly, but if you focus, it begins again and builds momentum.

To start a mobilization movement you have to be a dreamer. You can start dreaming again by remembering several fundamentals of dreaming and envisioning.
1. You are never too old.
2. Dreams and vision are always about improving life.
3. Dream with fellow dreamers.
4. Your dreams will encourage you.
5. Dreaming gives us the life-giving energy of hope.
6. When you dream you take risks.
7. You may lead others to help fulfill your dream.
8. You must have courage.
9. You cannot hold back.
10. Dreams and vision fuel action.

As our founder, I (Nolen) had a dream as well. My dream was to help Christians discover and engage in God's purposes for their lives. As an Executive Pastor of several mega-churches, I looked out at the congregation week after week, seeing tremendous latent talent that was not being directed toward any kind of kingdom work. I decided, that if I was going to impact people so they would become engaged in meaningful service, I would have to make a major adjustment in my life. I decided to leave the security of my church position and by faith work with individuals to help them discover and engage in their life purposes.

More than 10 years have passed and the results have been spectacular:

- Thousands of churches planted globally
- Thousands of people reached with the Gospel of Jesus Christ
- Thousands of copies of scripture distributed
- Thousands of Christian leaders trained around the world
- Thousands of impoverished people receiving food, clean water, clothing and shelter
- Thousands of at-risk children prepared for success in life
- Orphanages, churches, schools, hospitals and medical clinics built

Well known pastor Andy Stanley has said, "Missing out on God's plan for our lives must be the greatest tragedy this side of eternity." But it doesn't have to be that way. People can discover and fulfill God's purpose and mission for their lives. Churches and organizations can mobilize hundreds of people for significant ministry in the Kingdom of God.

Start dreaming and see if your vision is similar to ours. We envision:

- Hundreds of thousands of people discovering who they are – how God has shaped them for mission.
- Hundreds of thousands of people discovering and engaging in their God-given missions or purposes in life.
- Hundreds of millions of dollars mobilized to facilitate the fulfillment of these God-given missions.
- Millions reached for Christ and the basic humanitarian needs of millions met.

We know this is a reliable vision and God's plan because Ephesians 2:10 says everyone is called to bring glory to God by completing the good works that God designed beforehand for us to do. That means everyone. No exceptions. The missing component is experienced visionary leaders who will mobilize the thousands who today also have stopped dreaming and lack a vision of God's preferred future for their lives. What is needed are people whose vision is to wake up those who have become content with their engagement in Kingdom work having been relegated only to perhaps a Sunday service. We call these visionary leaders mobilizers. We hope you are one!

Take Away: Having a clear vision for mobilizing others will motivate and sustain you as you do the hard work of starting a mobilization movement.

Then he said to his disciples, "The harvest is plentiful but the workers are few. Ask the Lord of the harvest, therefore, to send out workers into his harvest field."
Matthew 9:37-38 (NIV)

Chapter 2
What is the Objective of a Mobilization Movement?

We know that the chief end of man is to bring glory to God. So how do we, as flawed people, do this? We do it by God's grace, flaws and all. Rick Warren states, "You will never be able to fulfill God's purpose for you until you understand that you are a complex and uniquely flawed individual who has been prepared for God's purposes. The question then is this, what do you do with the hand you are dealt."

We believe, that as far as mobilization is concerned, that the workers are plentiful but they lack motivation and direction. There is a great harvest of Christians who are ready to be mobilized and engage in meaningful service for others. The role of the mobilization movement is to organize, instruct, direct, encourage, release and stand by people as they impact others with the gospel. (We describe this at length in the next chapter.) There are hundreds of thousands of highly qualified individuals with passions, experiences and giftedness who are waiting to be awakened. They want to know how God has made them and their unique talents and abilities.

They want to discover their calling. When asked the question, "Why did God put me here on this earth?" they want to have a ready answer. Here are some excerpts from Author John Piper that help to describe the ultimate objective for a mobilization movement.

> The Scriptures teach throughout that all the works of God have as their ultimate goal the display of God's glory.

> The term "glory of God" in the Bible refers in general to the beauty of God's manifold perfections. It is an attempt to put into words what God is like in his magnificence and purity. It refers to his fullness of all that is good. The term might focus on his different attributes from time to time, like his power and wisdom and mercy and justice, because each one is awesome in its magnitude and quality. But in general God's glory is the perfect harmony of all his attributes into one infinitely beautiful being.

> God was not seeking glory which he lacked when he created man. Rather he was moved by a disposition to display or manifest himself. Like a full fountain has a tendency to overflow in streams of water, so God has a tendency to extend his glory beyond himself. God's goal, therefore, in created

man was to *display* his glory to and through man. Thus God's supreme goal in history, in all that he does from beginning to end, is to display his glory and bring honor and praise to his great name.

In view of what we now know about our Father's goal, what should be our response as faithful children? The *Westminster Shorter Catechism* asks, "What is the chief end of man?" That is, in view of God's goal what should ours be? It answers, "The chief end of man is to glorify God and to enjoy him forever." That sentence can scarcely be improved upon, for that is just what the Bible teaches. But what it means to glorify God and how one does it is not obvious to everybody.

One grave misunderstanding of what it means to glorify God would be to think that God is more glorious if we respond to him one way and less glorious if we respond to him another. God is not dependent upon man for the perfect display of his glory.

The supreme goal of God in history from beginning to end is the manifestation of his great glory. Accordingly, our duty is to bring our thoughts, affections, and actions into line with this goal. It should become our own goal. To join God in this goal is called glorifying God. The way we glorify God is first to delight in his glory more than in anything else and be grateful for it. Then, as a natural result of this joy in God, we experience freedom from selfishness and are moved to seek the good of others.

Our best example of giving glory to God is Jesus himself. John 17: 1-5 illustrates this.

> "When Jesus had spoken these words, he lifted up his eyes to heaven, and said, 'Father, the hour has come; glorify your Son that the Son may glorify you, since you have given him authority over all flesh, to give eternal life to all whom you have given him. And this is eternal life, that they know you the only true God, and Jesus Christ whom you have sent. *I glorified you on earth, having accomplished the work that you gave me to do.* And now, Father, glorify me in your own presence with the glory that I had with you before the world existed.'"

Jesus brought glory to God by completing the good work that God had for Him to do while He was here on the earth. He accomplished God's purpose for His life. He knew what God's purpose for Him was, and He was fully engaged in accomplishing that purpose.

The fundamental characteristic of a mobilization movement is exactly the same as it was for Christ...to bring glory to God. Just like Christ's example, mobilizing Christians to complete the good works God planned for them brings glory to God. A mobilization movement glorifies God by organizing, instructing, directing, encouraging, releasing and standing by people to accomplish their Ephesians 2:10 callings.

Take Away: The objective of everything should be glorifying God. We bring glory to God by bringing our dreams, objectives and actions in line with Him. Doing this frees us from self-will and makes it possible to bring Him glory as we fulfill our purposes.

Don't you have a saying, "It's still four months until harvest"? I tell you, open your eyes and look at the fields! They are ripe for harvest. John 4:35 (NIV)

Chapter 3
Why Do We Need Mobilization Movements?

Have you ever been surprised to learn of a need that existed in your community? It has happened to me (George). I was participating in a meeting concerning hunger in my community. As I live in a more affluent part of town I was not confronted with the hungry and assumed they lived "over there" somewhere. The leader of the meeting began to describe school children coming to school on Mondays with ravenous appetites. Because of their economic condition they qualified for a free breakfast to start the school day. On Monday, however, they would sneak through the line twice (with the school's full knowledge) to get a second portion. They had not had much to eat over the weekend. I was saddened that these children had been hungry all weekend and my heart went out to them. Then I got the shock of my life. The speaker revealed the location of the school. It wasn't "over there" it was less than a mile from my home! I had no idea that such a need existed so close to my home.

There are at least two reasons why we need mobilization movements. The first is the unaddressed needs in our communities and throughout the world and to show the love of Christ. The second is that Christians need help discovering and engaging in God's purposes for their lives.

Let's first look at the unaddressed needs. Did you know that:

- Most of the people on the face of the earth (66%) do not know Christ. That is estimated to be 4.7 billion who are without hope.
- Nearly one third (28%) of all human beings have never heard the Gospel.
- Poverty is a daily reality for most of the world. It is estimated that 1.2 billion men, women and children live in dire poverty.
- Clean drinking water is even a bigger problem as 1.4 billion do not have a source of clean water.
- An even larger problem is the lack of medical care. 1.5 billion have never had access to a doctor or health professional.
- Over one billion people do not have a roof over their heads. 1.7 billion people are without housing or shelter.
- Daily hunger (not to mention good nutrition) is the day after day reality for over 800 million people around the world.

Now let's focus a bit closer to home. Here are more staggering areas of need.

- Poverty among low income senior citizens is at epidemic proportion and getting worse. These folks have to decide between skipping meals and buying prescription medicines.
- The new poor are 50-plus men displaced from their jobs by the "great recession." Food pantries report a dramatic increase in this age group seeking assistance.
- Children are growing up without any supervision after school. While good works have sprung up in some communities to provide safety and training, most areas lack this needed resource.
- Even those who appear successful are actually medicated and still depressed. They live one paycheck away from financial disaster with a deep, gnawing sense that what was the American dream has vanished. What is worse is that they are completely disconnected from any relationship or resource that could encourage and direct improvements in their lives.

We suspect that you could also fill many pages with unmet needs you are aware of in your own community and around the world.

The second reason for needing mobilization movements is that there are few models where people are being effectively trained and encouraged to have a significant impact in their communities and the world. Through our experience of mobilizing others, we have learned that

14

Christians need help to discover and engage in God's purposes for their lives.

As we pointed our earlier, it is the job of the mobilization movement to organize, instruct, direct, encourage, release and then stand by people who are engaging in the activities that God uniquely created them to do.

Mobilizers organize in two ways. First, mobilizers promote the reality that people can discover their life purposes. By doing so, they become aware of those in their circles of relationships who have a desire to learn more. Second, mobilizers become aware of the needs of their community and around the world and the good works that already exist and are making an impact. This becomes valuable information when they later direct people to ways for becoming active in helping others.

Next, they provide instruction to unlock the God-given purposes inside those they serve. Many have begun utilizing *The GPS Life Journey* curriculum that we will describe at length in chapter seven. Once the eight week, facilitator-led curriculum is completed, they coach and gently direct people to focus on their strengths and become active in a capacity of service that is a perfect fit for them.

They also provide encouragement when the way forward is unclear or someone they are working with faces a roadblock. Finally, they both release and stand by those they mobilize.

A local mobilization movement harnesses resources (people) and directs them to engage in the good works that scripture tells us were designed for them before they were born. Not just any work, but the exact work God designed for them. The movement also helps people discover how God has uniquely gifted them and finally gives them a deep sense of significance. Now they can answer the question, "Why did God put me here on this earth?" with confidence and they live a meaningful life. They have become fulfilled individuals who are changing the world.

Take Away: There are needs all around us that we do not even know exist. Starting a mobilization movement in your community will produce focused people who are identifying and serving the needs of others.

And who knows
but that you have come to
your royal position
for such a time as this?" Esther 4:14b

Chapter 4
What Kind of Person Starts a Mobilization Movement?

Mobilizers come from all walks of life. Some discover the need for mobilization all on their own. Some are inspired by someone who mobilized them. They can be young, old or anywhere in between. Some are well-off financially and some have very little themselves. There are those with full-time jobs and some are retired. When it comes to mobilization, there are no socioeconomic barriers. Everyone has God given purposes and everyone can be mobilized.

Yet mobilizers need to possess four fundamental attributes to successfully start a mobilization movement in their community or church.

First, a person who starts a mobilization movement believes that we have a God-given general life purpose. As we read earlier, that general purpose is that we bring glory to God. We accomplish this by delighting in His glory more than in anything else in life. Again, John Piper makes God's glory relatable when he writes, "...in the Bible, I don't know of any truth that is more fundamentally pervasive than God's zeal to be glorified, which means His zeal for us so to think, so to feel, and so to act as to make him look as glorious as He is. We want to make God's glory shine. We want to make it visible."

Second, a person who starts a mobilization movement believes that everyone has a God-given specific purpose. We believe that God has a special purpose for each of us for which we have been uniquely equipped. We learn this in the Bible in the Apostle Paul's letter to the Ephesians. Most followers of Jesus Christ are familiar with Ephesians 2:8–9, where Paul declares we receive the salvation of God by grace through faith. Yet most followers of Christ are not familiar with Ephesians 2:10, which tells us, "We are the workmanship of Jesus Christ, created in Christ Jesus for good works, which God prepared beforehand, that we should walk in them." We are created to carry out these good works that God prepared for us, even before we were born!

Third, a person who starts a mobilization movement believes that God has called them to be a mobilizer. Calling is a very personal and spiritual thing. Approximately 15% of people who participate in a *GPS Life Journey* small group conclude that God wants them to help others discover and engage in their life purposes.

There are no special credentials necessary for those whom God calls. God has called people throughout time –

imperfect people, those who had made mistakes and those who had no idea what they were getting into. However, through God's grace we know that God invites us to serve and then shows us the way to follow. We are not perfect; we don't have all the answers; but we know that we belong to God and that God calls each of us by name.

Fourth, mobilizers are very passionate about what they do. An example of a passionate, ordinary person who was called to great service was Harriet Tubman. Her passion was about freeing slaves and woman's suffrage. She wrote, "Every great dream begins with a dreamer. Always remember, you have within you the strength, the patience, and the passion to reach for the stars to change the world." It was through the pain of being beaten by her masters as a slave child that she recognized her passions. Tubman carried physical and mental trama from those experiences into adulthood. She could have used her handicaps as an excuse not to act but she did not. In her case it was pain that produced passion and purpose, which drove her to be an advocate for the oppressed. Like Harriet, we all have the possibility to live a passionate and purposeful life. Most people discover that it is a combination of the joys and heartaches of life that form their passions.

Are you passionate about helping people make a difference in the world? Do you want to help others to know how they are a unique creation and what God put them here on earth to do? Do you want to help people discover and engage in their life purposes? That is what we are passionate about. We want to help people:

- understand how God has uniquely created and gifted them.
- discover and engage in His special purposes for their lives.
- find ways to serve others using their God-given profiles.
- have a sense of significance in their lives.
- begin leaving a legacy of impact for others.

If your passion is similar to our passion, then you too are a mobilizer!

Take Away: **People start mobilization movements because they have been called by God to mobilize others. They believe that every Christian has God-designed life purposes and mobilizers are passionate about seeing these gifts released for the benefit and impact of others.**

God called the light "day,"
and the darkness he called "night."
And there was evening, and there was
morning—the first day. Genesis 1:5 (NIV)

Chapter 5
What are the First Steps for Starting a Mobilization Movement?

If you are still reading then perhaps you feel a calling to start mobilizing others to change the world. If that is the case, you are also probably excited about the prospect of impacting the lives of people, seeing needs met and Christ's love demonstrated. If that describes you, then your next question would likely be, "How do I get started?" Let us give you a roadmap that is a result of what we have learned helping people like you to start mobilizing others.

The first thing you will need is a process and a curriculum that you can use to transition people from being bodies on a church pew to alive individuals who are impacting their community and perhaps the world. We published the *GPS Life Journey* because we could not find a product that did the job of mobilizing others completely. Certainly many good books and Bible studies have been written on how to discover and live lives with purpose. However, we observed that while people got excited about the prospect, few actually became active in fulfilling their life purposes. Our recommendation to you is that your first step is to take *The GPS Life Journey* yourself and become trained as a Certified *GPS Life Journey* Facilitator.

Next, you need to further develop your skills as a mobilizer. Here are several resources that we have found helpful in our own journey of becoming mobilizers. You should:

1. Participate in a small group study of *Experiencing God* by Henry and Richard Blackaby.

2. Read *Purpose* by Nolen Rollins.

3. Become familiar with the other major *GPS Life Journey* resources. Also, have extra copies that you can give away. These include:
- *Don't Waste Your Life* by John Piper
- *Finishing Well* by Bob Buford
- *From Success to Significance* by Lloyd Reeb
- *Glocalization* by Bob Roberts, Jr.
- *Halftime* by Bob Buford
- *Purpose Driven Life* by Rick Warren
- *Out Live Your Life* by Max Lucado
- *The Second Half* by Lloyd Reeb
- *Journey* by George Gundlach

4. Focus on your personal spiritual life and an intimate relationship with Jesus Christ. Mobilization is a highly

spiritual work. It can only be accomplished out of spiritual overflow. Those who attempt such an endeavor will certainly burn-out without a close relationship with Christ.

5. Develop a list of prospective individuals for participating in the *GPS Life Journey* Small Group. Who are these people? First remember that you cannot push people onto the mobilization path. Not everyone is ready for this journey, but those who are ready are easily led on the journey. The secret to enlisting people for the *GPS Life Journey* is to invite those who are yearning for the trip and desire the end destination.

We originally believed that the target audience was retired or semi-retired persons, who had plenty of time, resources, and abilities to make a difference. That is not true. Yes, there are many in this demography that are ready. But, there are even more in this group who are focused on the so-called American dream. They want to enjoy life – live it up in their multiple homes, drive their expensive automobiles, take exotic vacations, play golf and tennis, walk the white sand beaches and collect sea shells. These individuals have to come to the realization that this American dream for many becomes an empty nightmare.

Over the past several years we have discovered that there are people of all ages and walks of life that are ready. They want to make a difference. They want to leave a legacy. They want to change the world. They want to know and pursue God's purposes for their lives.

They are students who want their entire life to count for something important. They are not content to "sell their soul to the company store'" now and seek to undo the damage in their retirement. They are willing to sacrifice for the sake of the Kingdom.

They are blue-collar workers who realize that they can use their trade skills to contribute to the needs of people all around the world, as well as just down the streets where they live. They can build houses, clinics and churches. They can train underprivileged children. They can mentor students as they teach them how to play soccer and basketball.

They are doctors and medical technicians who want to provide health and nutrition to the sick and diseased in the slums of the world. They are teachers who want to provide a basic education for everyone no matter where they live. They are lawyers and accountants who help senior adults and migrant workers with legal issues.

They are business owners and entrepreneurs who want to assist business development in the impoverished regions of the world. They are managers and business leaders who desire to develop leadership skills and better business practices in countries with little leadership training. They are donors to business micro-loan funds in developing nations.

They are all around us every day. Mobilizers must develop the skills necessary to spot them. Mobilizers must also spread the word – throw out the bait and see which fish bite. It will be those who are hungry for something different. But remember, we can't push them. We can't force them to want it. When they are ready, they will jump into the boat on their own! You will be amazed, in time, at how many prospects for mobilization will find you, rather than your finding them.

6. Meet with individuals one-on-one and encourage their participation in *The GPS Life Journey* Small Group. Most people become attracted to discovering their life purpose through a mentoring relationship. Essentially you will tell them your story which will encourage them to see that they can discover their life purposes too.

7. Invite prospects to a mobilization vision-casting activity. Vision casting can take place in a home or larger venue. Here you bring together multiple prospects and share as well as encourage them to interact with each other.

8. Stay in touch with prospective participants. Follow-up is critical. Becoming mobilized is a big commitment and generally takes several contacts for people to become engaged.

9. Many prospects will want to take the *GPS Life Journey* after reading *Purpose* by Nolen Rollins. *Purpose* was written with the specific intent to make prospects want to discover and fulfill their life purpose. *Purpose* is available to Certified *GPS Life Journey* Facilitators at a discounted rate.

10. Participate in the *GPS Life Journey* Coach Workshop. Your effectiveness in becoming the best mobilizer that you can be will be enhanced though your knowledge of coaching. Our coaching curriculum is specifically designed for the benefit *GPS Life Journey* Facilitators.

11. There are many effective ways to connect with people and get the word out about mobilization. If you use *The GPS Life Journey* as your curriculum you can use resources available from Kingdom Mobilization such *GPS Life Journey* Brochures, *GPS* Ad Cards/Business Cards, *GPS Life Journey* web site, *GPS* Social Media – Facebook, Twitter, Blogs, Etc. and the Kingdom Mobilization web site.

12. Remember that the most powerful tool you have for starting a mobilization movement is your own story and those of others who have engaged in the process. Have both a long version of your story that you could share over a meal as well as a three minutes and a thirty seconds version for brief encounters.

This is some of what we have learned in our first decade of mobilizing believers. We also want to learn what works for you so we can share it with other mobilizers. One thing is certain, being prepared and following these steps will increase the impact of your mobilization efforts.

Take Away: Strengthen yourself by studying the numerous materials available on mobilizing. Next, seek prospects and stay connected to them.

...turning your ear to wisdom
and apply your heart to understanding...
Proverbs 2:2 (NIV)

Chapter 6
What Are the "Best Practices" of Mobilizing?

We have been actively engaged in mobilizing individuals and helping others start local mobilization movements for over 10 years. Because no manual existed when we began, we did a lot of experimenting. We did some things right and some things wrong. We want to provide you with the benefit of our experience so that your path to mobilization can be as smooth as possible.

<u>Mobilization Best Practices:</u>

Practice Mobilization Multiplication - When many are trained a movement begins. As you mobilize others, keep in mind that some of them will find a call to be mobilizers as well. This multiplication process will produce a mobilization movement in your community.

Collaborate - Join with those who have experience with mobilizing. There is a lot you can learn from them that will improve your success in mobilizing others.

Your Relationship with Christ – Remember that mobilization is a calling. Be sure to spend time reading the Bible and in prayer. We also recommend that you participate in an accountability relationship. It is a vital relationship with Jesus Christ that is essential to advance your mobilization movement.

Have a Board of Advisors – Do not go it alone. As soon as you identify several people in your community that are also passionate about mobilization, ask then to serve on an informal committee for advice, prayer and support. Consider establishing a Leadership Team, Board of Advisors and/or Board of Influence.

Don't Rush the Process – Mobilizing someone is a process or a journey. You cannot motivate individuals to pursue their life mission. They have to come to the position of being internally motivated by the circumstances of their lives.

High Capacity People - Extremely high capacity individuals are extremely guarded. They mostly believe that people want relationship with them in order to get something from them. Take it slow with these folks and let them initiate as much as possible. In time you will develop trust. The best way to engage individuals is through peer relationships (other extremely high capacity individuals).

Money Follows Mission – If fundraising for mobilization is part of your plan, remember that money follows mission.

It is a person's understanding and passion for the mission that motivates them to give to a cause. When people are motivated to engage in mission, their resources follow their mission.

Mobilization Is About the Now – No human knows what tomorrow will look like. Mobilization is for the "next stage of life" and may not be for the "rest of life." Individuals may experience a mission for several "next stages of life."

Mission Possible - The most difficult part of the mobilization process is "discovering" mission, not "engaging" in mission. Most individuals need coaching in discovering mission. We believe that every Christian should have a written mission statement that describes why God put them here on this earth.

Do It Together – If you are married, the mobilization journey is best when taken by couples. In many cases time commitment changes and financial adjustments are necessary to accomplish a life purpose. In these circumstances, it is critical that both husband and wife are in agreement. When they go through the mobilization process together a deep unity of purpose develops. We have found that small group gatherings are most effective when both spouses participate.

All People Are Possibilities - The mobilization audience is all ages, not just retired individuals. We have mobilized people from age 16 to age 85. Laborers, blue or white caller workers, professionals, and rich or poor alike are candidates to be mobilized.

People Are Different – Do not assume that everyone's motivation for mobilization is the same. Our experience is that the older generation is interested in moving from success to living a life of significance. On the other hand, the younger generations desire to get it right throughout life rather than pursuing purpose after success.

Give God the Glory He Is Due - The primary motivation for mobilizing others must be to bring glory to God. Our motivation cannot be merely meeting needs and helping individuals engage in mission and ministry. We need to keep the bigger picture of bringing glory to God ever present in our thinking.

Ask Questions - Learn to lead by asking good questions. When we are mobilizing others, we never want to be in the position of dictating direction. Our job is to help people understand the passions and motivations that God has placed inside of them.

Your Lips Are Sealed - Keep confidential everything that should be kept confidential. Enough said.

Coach - Mobilization is not "product" driven but "coach" driven. Most people cannot discover and engage in their life mission without coaching. Great mobilizers need formal coach training.

Be a Prospector – Your prospecting list is one of your most valuable resources. Every time you connect with someone new always get their full name, phone number and email address.

Real Life Stories – The most powerful tool in helping people to become mobilized are real life stories of successful mobilizations. Start with your story and tell it often. Soon you will have stories from those you have helped mobilize that you can tell as well.

Experiment – Once someone is mobilized and has an idea of how they might get involved in significant service, encourage them to test their conviction. As an example, if someone feels called to mentor teenagers suggest they spend time with teens at an after school program for latch key kids. If someone feels a call to comfort the elderly suggest they begin by visiting a retirement home. There are thousands of opportunities to test what they believe they are called to. This practice is a great way to prove where God is leading.

Study Success – Before starting your mobilization movement, take time to study other successful movements. We can connect you with others, from whom you can learn, because they are farther along in the process.

Attend Workshops – Kingdom Mobilization offers periodic Best Practices Workshops. Take advantage of these and other opportunities to learn.

Connect – The Kingdom Mobilization staff stands ready to help you. Connect with us at any time.

GPS Life Journey Facilitator Best Practices:

Stay in Character - Remember, you are a facilitator, not a teacher or instructor. There is a big difference. Think of yourself as a guide leading others on their own journey of discovery.

Take Charge and Lead - Control the amount of time for fellowship at the beginning of sessions. Also, limit non-essential conversation within sessions. Sometimes you will have a "real talker" in your group and will just have to graciously move the group forward. If it becomes a real problem privately ask the person to help you keep the group on track.

Eat Elsewhere – Meals are not recommended as part of a *GPS Life Journey* small group. Snacks are OK but not necessary.

Meeting Schedule – While a group may meet weekly, every other week, or monthly our experience is that weekly is better. The day and time of each session may be set according to the facilitator's schedule or may be determined by what day and time is most suitable for the group.

Make-Up Sessions – On occasion someone will miss a session. The most effective way for them to make it up is to have them meet with you one hour early before the next session.

Plan Your Time - Allocate time for responses, assessments, questions, comments, and in–session assignments. Allocate time and make sure everyone understands the homework assignment for the next session.

Know Them - Know the personal profile of each member of your group. Involve individuals in accordance with his/her preferred environment for learning.

Be Creative - Use a variety of learning methods – small group interaction, visual aids, etc.

Help Between Sessions - Schedule one-on-one coaching appointments with each individual or couple as needed.

Accountability - Hold group members accountable for all assignments. Remind them of assignments with regular emails.

Leave Room for Prayer – Mobilizing others is a very spiritual process. Without the intervention of the Holy Spirit you will not get very far. Begin and end each session with an appropriate prayer for the goals of the session.

Be Prepared – Have a supply of *GPS Life Journey* Workbooks and other resources such as markers and large poster pages on hand.

Cast Vision – Whether with a group or one-on-one, conduct vision-casting sessions to enlist GPS participants.

Do a pilot – A great way to introduce the *GPS Life Journey* to a church or other organization is to conduct an eight session pilot group with key personnel. This will achieve their "buy in" and enable you to impact the entire organization.

Do a Blitz – An effective way to begin GPS in a new location is to conduct a GPS Blitz. Key individuals spend two intensive days taking *The GPS Life Journey* and a third day being trained to be GPS Facilitators. All homework assignments are completed before the GPS Blitz.

Multiply – Once you have taken a few people through GPS identify those who would like to facilitate their own groups. Multiply yourself by conducting a *GPS Life Journey* Facilitator Workshop.

Stay in Touch – Stay connected to your GPS graduates by holding periodic GPS graduate reunions. These are times for people to share their successes as well as receive encouragement when they encounter a road-block.

While we have learned a great deal we are still learning. Nearly every day we continue to fine-tune the process. We will continue to share best practices to everyone who walks with us on this mobilization journey.

Take Away: Start mobilizing using the tested practices we have discovered over the last decade.

*Do your best to present yourself to God
as one approved, a worker who does not
need to be ashamed and who correctly
handles the word of truth. 2 Timothy 2:15 (NIV)*

Chapter 7
How the *GPS Life Journey* Helps You Mobilize Others

The GPS Life Journey is published by Kingdom Mobilization, a leader in helping start mobilization movements. We have been mobilizing people for kingdom service and training and coaching others to begin local mobilization movements for over a decade. We mobilize men and women for good works by helping individuals:
- have a sense of significance or fulfillment.
- leave a legacy of importance.
- meet the needs of other people.
- have community or global impact.
- use their God-given resources and gifts wisely.

The GPS Life Journey curriculum is our primary resource for helping Christians discover how God has made them and begin living a life of significance. This is most often accomplished through *GPS Life Journey* small groups.

We invite people on a journey to discover God's specific plan for their life. We show them how they are created with unique gifts and abilities that He wants them to use? Participants see how God wants them to make a difference in the world. Finally, they understand how they have been designed for a special purpose that God wants them to understand and to fulfill in their lifetime.

The GPS Life Journey is not merely a book, a conference, a seminar or a course. It is a journey ... a process, which helps you discover and engage in God's special purpose for your life. It is a lifelong journey. As you fulfill God's purpose for the next stage of your life, God is preparing you for even another mission on your journey.

Participation in *The GPS Life Journey* helps people...
- Understand how God has uniquely created them.
- Discover His special purpose for their lives.
- Engage in fulfilling that purpose.
- Serve others using their God-given profile.
- Have a sense of significance in their lives.
- Make a difference in the world.
- Leave a legacy of impact for others.

The basic goal of *The GPS Life Journey* is to help participants discover their God-given purpose for the next stage of their lives and engage in fulfilling those purposes. *The GPS Life Journey* consists of eight ninety minutes sessions ...
1. Discovering My Personality
2. Discovering My Experiences, Abilities and Strengths
3. Discovering My Passions, Spiritual Gifts and Values

4. Discovering How to Get Direction from God
5. Developing My Personal Mission Statement
6. Developing My Personal Vision
7. Developing Priority Action Steps and Venues
8. Developing Margin in My Life

Once participants complete *The GPS Life Journey* curriculum they have developed a written road map with specific definitions and answers for 15 key areas:

1. My Personality Type
2. Things I Do Best Based on My Experiences
3. My Greatest Natural Abilities and Skills
4. My Greatest Strengths
5. My Greatest Passions and Interests
6. My Primary Spiritual Gifts
7. My Personal Core Values
8. Direction/Messages from God
9. My Personal Mission Statement
10. Vision for the Next Stage of My Life
11. Priority Action Steps for the Next Stage of My Life
12. Personal Ministry Venue(s) for the Next Stage of My Life (Team and Position)
13. Time Margin for the Next Stage of My Life
14. Financial Margin for the Next Stage of My Life
15. Spiritual Margin for the Next Stage of My Life

For people who complete *The GPS Life Journey* and feel called to mobilize others, we also offer *The GPS Life Journey Facilitator Workshop*. This workshop trains *GPS* graduates to conduct and facilitate their own *GPS Life Journey* groups.

Another opportunity is for people to become GPS Coaches. We provide this training through *The GPS Life Journey Coach Workshop*. This workshop equips people to do one-on-one life purpose coaching. The *GPS Life Journey Coach Certification* certifies you to coach individuals on their *GPS Life Journey*.

Utilizing *The GPS Life Journey* and our other resources will help you mobilize others and change the world.

Take Away: Use *The GPS Life Journey Workbook* as your central mobilization curriculum.

Not that I have already obtained all this, or have already
arrived at my goal,
but I press on to take hold of that
for which Christ Jesus took hold of me. Philippians 3:12-14
(NIV)

Chapter 8

Mobilization Stories - In Their Own Words

Mobilization is life-changing! There are many individuals currently engaged in carrying out their God-given life purposes all around the world as a result of *The GPS Life Journey* process. They are having a huge impact in the Kingdom of God.

The hungry are being fed. The sick and diseased are receiving medical care. The naked are being clothed. Widows and orphans are being cared for in the name of Jesus. Water wells are being dug in barren places. The gospel of Jesus Christ is being shared. People are receiving the salvation of Christ. Churches are being planted. Pastors and church leaders are being trained. Local benevolence ministries are meeting the needs of the poor and underprivileged. Women and children are being rescued from human trafficking. Children in the world's largest slums are being educated. University students are being equipped for success in life. Businesspersons and professionals in developing nations are being challenged to meet the needs of the people in their communities.

Here are several stories from people who have been mobilized by participating in a *GPS Life Journey* process.

Don Gunther (Former Executive of Global Corporation)

I was fortunate to have a significant level of business success throughout the world. I spent 40 years with the Bechtel Group, the world's leading engineering and construction firm. We worked in 120 countries, engineering and building some the most complicated and largest structures that were ever constructed. In the later stage of my career, the Engineer and Construction Society awarded me the best executive award for the 1990's. When I retired, I was Vice Chairman and was responsible for all of our business units around the world. I thoroughly enjoyed my career with Bechtel.

I tried retirement with the big house and the big boat but soon realized I needed to contribute back more. With some friends, I got heavily involved with the Naples Wine Festival and we raised over 100 million dollars for the charities emphasizing help for the abused and abandoned children. In 2009, I also joined the board of the Immokalee Foundation which helps the impoverished migrant children of Immokalee, Florida to improve their education and help them find a suitable career plan and a job.

Although I was contributing my leadership time to my golf club and my community association and to two other non-

profits, I still felt something was missing. That's when a friend introduced me to the GPS Life Journey. It all started with a question to me that asked me if I knew why God put me on this earth. The GPS Life Journey helped me focus on the skills I had and how I might use them to help others and increase my impact in the world. It helped me evaluate my strengths and weaknesses and through it, I began to identify where God would like to use me.

Coupled with my commitments to my family, I felt called to accept the Chairmanship of the Immokalee Foundation. I think we have improved the organization's focus and are improving the chance of success for about 800 children.

The GPS Life Journey was very significant in my finding and fulfilling my life purpose.

Dawn Birch (Professional Singer)
After taking the GPS Life Journey course, it is as though God turned over and reordered the puzzle pieces of my life and showed me who I am. I now have a heightened sense of His Holy Spirit working in the world and I am much more sensitive to the various situations and people He has positioned around me.

The GPS Life Journey helped me to understand, focus, sharpen and utilize all my unique God given personality traits, skills, gifts, and passions. Then I was able to take that knowledge and answer the question, "God, now what and why?"

I now understand why God gave me a 3-octave voice, a six-foot frame, and a platform to perform for literally thousands of influential people each year. It was not just for me to provide entertainment for the wealthy, pay my own bills, and enjoy a little bit of notoriety. Instead, it was to be a bold and faithful influence to my audiences of the grace and mercy of JEVOHAH God and persuade them to be reconciled to Him through His Son, Jesus the Christ. Over the years He has provided amazing avenues of influence for me. (From sometimes reaching thousands via newspaper articles, concerts, and "fan mail" to intimate one on one conversations with wardrobe designers.)

My personal relationship with Jesus has grown drastically since applying everything I have learned in the GPS Life Journey and it has also helped me see how others fit into God's plan. (How I wish my husband and I had taken this course years ago, as it would have saved us from many arguments ... but that's an entire other thesis.)
The GPS life journey has helped me to know myself and what I am to do while on this earth. I now look forward to the day, with hope, when God will say to me "Well done good and faithful servant," when I complete all He has planned for me to do while here on earth.

Doug Hodge (Retired CFO of Global Corporation)

Life has a way of happening without you ever realizing what's going on around you until you stop and listen. In 1977 I graduated from the University of Kentucky with an MBA and headed off to work in the financial field for an automotive parts manufacturer. I had conducted business in over 20 countries and managed billions of dollars in revenue. I was also a mentor to many young people in the corporate financial world.

Thirty-three years later God helped me to reevaluate my life. It is good to stop and listen. It started with hearing Nolen Rollins speak on God's Plan for Success (GPS) the weekend of July 4, 2010. From there I accepted God's invitation to pursue a second half to my life and then I spent the next couple months really understanding who Doug Hodge really was. In the fall of 2010 my wife and I joined a GPS Life Journey Small Group with four other couples and worked through the GPS Road Map together. My current mission statement is to provide training and mentoring for global business owners to enhance their Kingdom building abilities.

I was able to come to this statement by understanding my strengths and weaknesses, my personality, my gifts, my experiences and my abilities (all sessions of the GPS Life Journey). Then it was time to let go and let God help me understand what he desired me to do with the personal profile he had given me. For me this was the time I started to understand that my failures along with my successes, along with countless other experiences, were gifts from God to help me move into his plan for my life.

Working with Kingdom Mobilization I have been able to:
- *Train students and begin working with business owners in Russia.*
- *Train teachers, business owners, and ministry participants in India.*
- *Train and mentor business owners and ministry participants in Nigeria.*

Now, as I get ready to expand efforts, whether missions work, education, or work endeavors, I bounce it against my mission statement and if it moves it forward I proceed and if not I stop. Living life on mission with God is a blast!

Risa Baker (Business Owner/Operator)

My husband and I were already seeking to discover what God might have for the next stage of our lives when providentially we met Nolen Rollins, author of the GPS Life Journey. We started our GPS Life Journey soon thereafter. Since then my passion has been to share my GPS Life Journey experience with others. My mission, to influence and lead others to discover and engage in their life's purposes, has been evolving ever since.

God has given me amazing opportunities. First, I trained and became a GPS Life Journey Facilitator. Next came the opportunity to teach the first GPS Life Journey Small Group in Atlanta, GA. It is exciting to help others discover who they are and how God has made them and witness how God is giving abundant opportunities to engage in their passions.

Later I traveled to Nigeria and had the opportunity to train students, ministry leaders, and small business owners. Using The GPS Life Journey as their textbook, they learned how God has uniquely made them and they discovered the individual and unique missions God has for them. One Nigerian Business owner said to me, "I'm still so amazed at your total commitment to us and the great passion and love with which you taught us during the International GPS Summit which has greatly impacted my life and purpose."

I feel so privileged to be able to share the GPS Life Journey with others in the US and around the world. I love the success stories people are sharing. It's easy to be passionate about the mission God has given and equipped me to do. It is such a great blessing to make a difference in other's lives.

Take Away: People from all stations in life are being mobilized and finding God's purposes for the next stage of their lives. They are business people, teachers, healthcare workers, homemakers, maintenance men and the list goes on.

Mobilization Quick Reference Guide

Chronological Components of a Thriving Mobilization Movement

A healthy mobilization movement should be developed in an order similar to this.

1. Recognized area leader to provide overall coordination for the movement
2. Vison casting events to produce workshop participants, facilitators, leadership team prospects and micro movements:
    a. Impact Breakfasts and Luncheons
    b. After Work Hours Events for Professionals
    c. Church Leadership Presentations
    d. One-on-One Vision Casting
3. People completing the *GPS Life Journey*
4. Inflow of new Certified Facilitators to increase the movement's momentum

5. Facilitators forming and coaching new *GPS Life Journey* groups and/or Blitzes
6. Leadership Team to share the load and broaden the impact of the mobilization efforts
7. Flexible workshop formats:
    a. Eight Session Weekly Format
    b. Two-day Blitz Format
    c. One-one-One Format
    d. Custom Formats to Meet Unique Needs
8. Graduate engagement:
    a. Customer relationship management tool (CRM) to manage data concerning contacts and graduates
    b. Reunions to inspire and encourage graduates and prospects
    c. Communication to the movement at large through:
        - Newsletters via Mailchimp or Constant Contact
        - Blogs highlighting best practices
        - Twitter posts for encouragement to press on on the journey
    d. Mission Mentoring (GPS 2.0) for ongoing coaching through the *GPS* process
    e. Fund Raising to support the costs associated with the movement
9. Leadership that is well connected and can advise graduates regarding engagement opportunities
10. Leadership that models success for coaching others who want to start their own area movements

Checklist for Beginning a Mobilization Movement In Your Church, City or Region

- Participate in a GPS Life Journey Small Group or Blitz.
- Complete your Personal GPS Life Journey Road Map (15 Steps).
- Compose your Personal GPS Life Journey Story (short and long versions).
- Participate in the GPS Life Journey Facilitator Workshop.
- Participate in the GPS Life Journey Coach Workshop.
- Read the Mobilize Manual (Understanding Mobilization and Starting Your Local Movement).
- Study the model of other mobilization movements in other churches, cities or regions.
- Read and encourage others to read *Purpose* by Nolen Rollins and *Journey* by George Gundlach.
- Become familiar with other mobilization resources.
- Order materials from Kingdom Mobilization to conduct a GPS Life Journey Small Group.
- Conduct vision-casting activities (groups or one-on-one) to enlist participants for *The GPS Life Journey* Small Group or Blitz
- Conduct a pilot GPS Life Journey Small Group or Blitz for 5-10 people.

- As soon as you identify other individuals who are passionate about mobilization, establish a local Leadership Team, an Advisory Board and/or a Board of Influence.
- Conduct a GPS Life Journey Facilitator Workshop after you have two or more individuals interested in becoming facilitators.
- Conduct periodic GPS Life Journey Graduate Reunions to stay in touch with and for accountability for graduates.
- Enlist leaders to begin other mobilization movements within your target area (especially if it is a city or regional movement).
- Contact Kingdom Mobilization staff as needed all along your journey.
- Attend the Mobilization Movements Best Practices Summits offered by Kingdom Mobilization.

We Would Like To Get To Know You
If you are passionate about helping people discover and engage in their life purposes and want to start your own local mobilization movement, we can help. We hope you will connect with us so together we can explore further what it means to be a mobilizer.

For more information or to contact us regarding Kingdom Mobilization or The GPS Life Journey consult either of our two websites. For mobilization go to www.kingmo.org. For *The GPS Life Journey* find us at www.GPSLifeJourney.com.

Contact the authors:
George Gundlach, george@kingmo.org
Nolen Rollins, nolen @ kingmo.org

Join with us in...
Helping men and women discover and engage in God's purposes for their lives. Together we can change the world.

www.ingramcontent.com/pod-product-compliance
Lightning Source LLC
Chambersburg PA
CBHW060539030426
42337CB00021B/4350